7 Video Marketing Secrets

How to Stop Burning Cash on Video
Productions and Shoot Amazing Viral
Videos

Erich M. Tolman

Table of Contents

Description

Whether your goal is to grow your YouTube channel or to utilize video marketing to increase your brand recognition, sell more products, and increase your social media presence *7 Video Marketing Secrets* can help.

It has been found that marketing has been improved by ninety-seven percent with the use of video. Not only does video allow you to reach a new audience than you previously could, but it is also easier to digest, increases search engine optimization, builds trustworthiness between brands and consumers, creates new opportunities for advertisements, and increases sales.

In an age of social media, people have gradually been placing less trust in traditional advertisements. But, while social media may negatively impact traditional ads, it also offers its own opportunities. To become a well-trusted brand in this era, it is essential to learn the ins and outs of these platforms and all the ways in which they can be used to promote and further your business.

If you are having trouble growing your YouTube channel or making use of video marketing, this book can help. You will learn the details of the seven secrets you need to improve your video marketing or grow your YouTube channel, plus more.

In This Book You Will Find:

- How to learn about your target audience

- Learn which type of humor to use for your viewer

- Find the best length of video for your platform

- How to keep your message simple

- Adding music to increase interesting

- Increasing humor with music

- Find your selling point, even if you aren't selling anything

- How to perfect your video through filming and editing

- How to find and hire a social media influencer

- *And more...*

Introduction

Video marketing is more popular than ever. In fact, YouTube reports that they receive over one-billion hours of video views in a single day. Video content is incredibly versatile, easy-to-digest, engaging, and accessible to a wide audience. Nearly everyone in modern countries has access to the internet, and therefore they are able to find and watch almost endless video content easily. While a picture may speak a thousand words, a video speaks much more. Whether you are a YouTube channel hoping to market yourself or a business owner, learning the art of video marketing can help expand your horizons and increase your opportunities.

There are some interesting statistics regarding video marketing. One of these statistics has shown that 97 % of video markets feel as if videos help their customers better understand and trust their product. 81 % of businesses are now utilizing video marketing. By the year 2021, over 80 % of all search engine traffic is estimated to be directed towards videos. Lastly, 90 % of customers claim that videos impact their purchase decisions. It is plain to see why video marketing is on the rise and has such extreme power over the success of a business.

While you may be able to film a short and quick video with a smartphone, nearly everyone can do it; these videos are often limited in the number of views they receive unless they are filmed or promoted by a celebrity. Thankfully, there are many secrets that you can use to make professional quality videos that will capture your audience; you only need to know how. In this book, you will learn seven of the top secrets in video marketing to help you excel, build your brand, reach a wider audience, and engage with your customers and viewers.

Chapter 1: Know Your Audience

When creating content of any type you need to care about the audience. This is especially true of video content, where people are likely to switch to another video within 15 s if you are unable to capture their interest.

Your video content should feel like a conversation. Yet, you are most likely going to be the only person talking, but you want to be engaging as if it were a conversation. Imagine you are talking to someone, you would get bored if they droned on and on about their kids, house, where they grew up, and their hobbies if they ignored you during the conversation. Nobody wants to talk to someone who makes them feel as if their opinions and ideas don't matter; it should be an equal exchange.

In order to create videos that can fully engage your viewers, adding value to their lives and impacting them so that they leave comments furthering the discussion, you first need to know your audience. This is one of the most important factors in successful video marketing, but also often forgotten.

You need to understand what the lives of your audience are like. What are they passionate about? What makes them laugh? What are they struggling with? If you can find the answers to these questions, then you can more directly impact the people who will be the most impacted by your content and products.

If you already have an idea of who your target audience might be, you may need to throw that idea out. Rather than assuming, it is important to find substantial evidence which you can trust. Try either conducting your own market research or going over industry reports from companies who should have a similar target audience. This is important, as our ideas of who the ideal audience for our product is can often be misconstrued.

After you have a general idea of who your audience is, you can begin to create an audience persona. This will outline the common trains in a typical viewer of your content, such as their characteristics and situations. Some examples of these details are geographic location, lifestyle factors, age, marital status, gender, household size, and what benefits they might be looking for in a product.

After you have assembled the outline for your viewership and their persona, then you need to conduct further research. In this stage, you want to conduct a quantitative study which asks specific questions on a large scale. Questions such as, "How is this product important to you?" and "What is your main consideration when buying these types of products?"

These studies can be conducted in-person, online, or over the phone. While they are perfect for anyone selling products or services, people who are using YouTube as the business can directly ask their viewers questions concerning the videos. Such as "why do you watch my channel" and "what do you consider when subscribing to a channel."

After collecting the data from a quantitative survey, try conducting a smaller survey in which you ask the participants to delve deeper into their thoughts and expand on how they feel further. While this step isn't absolutely necessary, you will find it will help you further understand your audience's psychological profile. The more you know your audience, the better you can target your videos and services toward them.

Analyze your competitors to find how your audience is reacting to their marketing and services, and how they then interact with their audience. Discovering what your competitor is doing successfully and why your target audience appreciates it can help you enhance yourself and possibly even improve on what they are doing.

Monitor and analyze not only any interaction with your audience but also use analytic tools to find all the details of how your audience has responded to your video. For instance, how many minutes of your footage did they watch? What demographics are they from? How did they find your video? YouTube and Facebook provide built-in analytic features, but you can find additional analytic programs and websites, as well.

Study the analytics and comments from your viewers over time, and use the knowledge you glean from it to improve your future videos. You want to continually be relearning what draws in your viewership, how long they stay for, and what keeps them coming back so that you can incorporate it into future videos.

Now that you have an idea of who your audience is before you ever film a video you want to have a clear idea what that video is supposed to speak to in the person. Are you trying to make them laugh, relate, or understand how you can resolve a problem of theirs? Sometimes videos can have two purposes, for instance, you might want to show them how your services can answer a problem of theirs but in an amusing way in order to make them laugh. You can choose multiple purposes, but try to keep it limited to two; you can always use other purposes in the following videos.

One great way to really grab your audience's attention is with humor. Even companies, who previously kept a more composed public image, have begun to add bits of humor into their advertisements. You just have to watch cable TV to see how many commercials utilize the tool of humor. This is especially true on Superbowl Sunday when every commercial is designed to be even more amusing than the last, trying to be visible in the sea of advertisements. Just because you are trying to be professional, does not mean you can't also entertain your audience. After all, people have a habit of tuning out informative videos; they want to be entertained.

There are many ways in which you can add a splash of humor, but however you choose, be sure that it does not take over your main talking point. Think about most popular comical commercials, they use humor to highlight the main focus, but not to overwhelm the   important   points. Some of the types of humor you can add include:

- Hyperbole
  This type of humor is based in reality but is an exaggeration that is not made to be taken literally. It needs a balance so that it is exaggerated enough to be funny, but so that it still feels real to the viewer. You want the viewer to be able to laugh along while relating to the situation and therefore how your product or service can help them.

- Timing
  while timing is important for any form of video marketing, it can also be used to inject visual humor. You can film something where it seems as if it is going to be completely straight-laced, only for at the last second for the viewer to see a twist in the visuals, something funny that they were not expecting.

- Farce
  while farce can be a lot of fun, it is important to know your audience well, as it does not amuse all viewers. This type of humor often includes absurd circumstances, buffoonery, and ridiculous characters.

- Deadpan
  If maybe it is a little challenging to pull off well, but deadpan humor is often quite popular when both scripted and acted well. In this type of humor, the person will often deliver straight truth along with some lines that become funny when they are said completely straight-faced, without a note of

humor. The lack of humor where it would usually be displayed is really what makes deadpan so amusing.

- Parody
  There is a reason that Saturday Night Live has become so popular, people can't get enough of parodies. This type of humor can often be utilized in order to poke fun at your competition, without directly naming them. But, you can also create parodies of famous pop culture. Just be sure that you are poking fun at these things without confrontationally attacking them. Otherwise, it could make your viewers feel uneasy.

- Metaphor, Puns, and Wordplay
  While metaphors, wordplay, and puns are all different, they greatly crossover in terms of humor. Whether you are comparing two like objects, taking advantage of two words which sound similar or combining two words together, you can add in hints of humor without giving your video an overall comical feel.

While adding humor is not always a necessity, if you want to engage your audience better and keep them hooked on your every word, then it is an option more than worth exploring. For instance, if you know your target audience is women in their 20's and 30's and your product is something to touch up their roots and dye job, then you can make light of the situation. Use hyperbole to lightly and sarcastically depict women who are running out of the house, only to be hit by the sudden realization of how their hair looks. But, if they have your product they have the ability to touch up their roots while on the go quickly.

Whether you are selling a product, your services, or your channel, you can add in humor to entertain your audience and keep them coming back for more.

Chapter 2: Keep It Short and Simple

"Focus on the first 10 seconds. If you look at your YouTube audience retention or Wistia stats you'll notice that approximately 20% of your viewers drop off in the first 10 seconds." — Brian Dean, Founder of Backlink

In our daily lives, we have TV, smartphones, radio, the internet, and much more all around us. This is continuing to shorten our concentration spans. If we find something boring a distraction is literally right at our fingertips. This means that your message is one of the millions constantly battling for attention. In order to reach your audience, maintain their focus, and leave an impression you have to get your message across in a short amount of time.

YouTube is the largest video sharing network and people's preferred platform. Some people may disagree with the wan in which the company handles some matters, specifically those regarding smaller channels and their ability to monetize videos, but it is still the best platform around. If you want to get high traffic, then YouTube is often the way to go.

While initially, YouTube will only allow you to upload videos of a maximum length of fifteen minutes if you verify your account in settings, you can then upload any video under twenty gigabytes. Some people may utilize this to post long keynote speeches or footage from conventions, but in general, you want to avoid this.

The most popular videos on YouTube tend to vary in length between forty-two seconds and nine minutes fifteen seconds. Out of these, the standard length of popular videos is regularly four minutes and eleven seconds. YouTube even has an option where people can filter their search results by either short videos (those under four minutes) or long videos (those longer than twenty minutes).

This means that while you can have a longer video; you are safer going with something around the four-minute mark.

Even with short videos, people will gradually drop off from viewing. One study found that over the length of a four to five-minute video less than sixty percent of your viewers will watch the entire video.

Yet, with a one to two-minute video, an average of seventy-five percent of people remained until the end. For this reason, it is important to stay energetic, speak clearly, get your message across, and hook your viewers quickly.

If you have a subject that you want to cover and require a long time to discuss, consider if you can discuss it in a series of mini-videos rather than a single long video. For instance, if you run a family-owned local pet store, rather than doing a single long video on the various dog grooming products you recommend, you can do a series of mini videos with each video recommending a single product. Once you upload the videos, you can then add them to a playlist for people to go through at their leisure. Not only is this better for search engine optimization, but it is easier for people with time constraints, those who might get otherwise distracted, and it makes the content more easily digested.

Most people are used to introducing calls to action, where you ask your viewers to follow an action such as subscribing, at the end of articles. But, when you are sharing a video on YouTube, you can do this at the beginning by using the editing features to add annotations and links. Having a visible non-verbal call to action at the beginning of your video will ensure that people who don't stick around have the opportunity to check out your product or services further. Although, you should still include a verbal and visible call to action at the end of your video, as well.

A number of both academic and scientific studies have been conducted on the number of shares videos receive and their commonalities. They found that the more emotion the video drew out from the person, it didn't matter whether or not it was a commercial or user-generated content, and the more likely they were to share it. This means the more the person laughed, felt hopeful, or cried the more likely they were to share it among their social network. This is why longer commercials indeed tend to play off of people's emotions. After all, thirty seconds is rarely enough time to have people make the emotional connection; it takes time.

While YouTube may be the leading video sharing social network and the go-to option when you want to utilize video marketing, there are other options as well, and it is best not to ignore them. You want to get your message to as wide of an audience as possible, and that means also posting videos on Facebook, Twitter, and Instagram but when you do this, be sure to share different content across all social media.

Otherwise, you might bore people who see the same content from you repeatedly on all your social networks. Give your audience a reason to follow you on all of these different platforms. It is best to customize the length of the video depending on the platform. While four minutes may be ideal on YouTube, one minute is better for Facebook, thirty seconds for Instagram, and forty-five seconds on Twitter according to market research and analytics.

Along with keeping your message short, you need to keep it simple. Rather than trying to cover multiple topics in one video, each video should contain only one topic. Not only will this help your audience stick around, but it will also improve your SEO, the number of views your channel receives, it makes it simpler for your viewers to find the information they need, and it will make it easier for your audience to remember what each video is about.

Another aspect of keeping a message simple is to keep it clear and concise. You don't want to drone on for long periods switching topics, or else your viewer will flip to another video before they even consciously consider it. You want your main point to be easy to understand, plainly spoken, and delivered in a way that remains direct yet entertaining.

Lastly, you want to ensure that you are trustworthy and that your video is credible. This means that not only do you need to share the truth with your viewers, but you need to believe it yourself. Even if you tell your audience the amazing aspects of your services which are true, if you don't fully believe it, neither will they. Be real, show them how people just like them can benefit from what you are offering, showcase your product or service work, and let them feel a connection to you not solely as a brand but as a person.

When you are posting a video, you should ask yourself not only if the message is relevant, if it targets the correct audience, or if impacts people emotionally. You also want to ask yourself if the video is of the correct length, if the message is paced well, if is it clear, and does it help people trust you?

Being short and simple may be more difficult than it first sounds, but mastering this will truly impact your videos for the better. You will find that once you utilize this secret, you will have an uptake in views and video interaction.

Chapter 3: Keep Them Engaged

While you may be talking in front of a camera when filming, you are not talking to the camera. It is important to remember that you are having a conversation, not a speech. Otherwise, your audience will feel as if you are only talking to hear your own voice, rather than to add value to their lives. Because of this, it has long been shown that one of the keys to keeping your viewers engaged is to interact with them. Yet, many people still don't know how to communicate with their audience. In this chapter, I will reveal the secrets to keeping your viewers engaged and creating a long-term loyal audience.

When your audience feels that they are heard and important it increases how invested they are in you, your brand, and your videos. This means that they are more likely to become loyal to you, watch all of your content, leave "likes" and share your content with their friends. It may be hard to find these loyal viewers in the beginning, after all, not many people will have heard of your channel yet. But, if you ask your family and friends to check out your channel, it will up your view count, likes, and comments. This, in turn, will help you rank higher in search results and help you gain a larger following.

Part of engaging your audience requires that they know what they are getting into. Nobody wants to spend their precious time watching a video when they have no idea if they will get what they desire out of it. If you mention at the beginning of the video what you will be discussing, it can help them know that they want to stick around. You can do this by saying something such as "in this video, we will be discussing the options on the market for cat food. By the end of this video, you will know exactly what to feed your cat for the healthiest diet."

It is important to remember that you are offering them a promise of what is to come in the video, and you must deliver. If you don't, then you will lose their trust. When filming, always keep in mind that your video is meant to be open dialogue and a conversation. To help promote further discussion and engagement from your viewers be sure that you keep your points clear, simple and easy to digest. You also want to emphasize important highlights, keep things light and amusing rather than giving a lecture, and when possible end the video by recapping any important points to help your audience remember.

We know that everyone has an opinion; this is made clear by social media. Your viewers will appreciate if you express a desire to know their opinion, rather than just telling them what you think. One way in which you can express this is by simply saying in your video how much you appreciate comments, likes, shares, and subscribers. This lets them know that you notice them, and it makes your video feel more personable.

Try to respond to your audience on various platforms. Even if you decide to use YouTube as your main video marketing location, don't solely respond to people in the comments. Take time to respond on Twitter, Instagram, Facebook, and any other social media sites you happen to be on. This will help get your videos out to a wider audience and help people who are less versed in YouTube to interact with you.

Comments, whether positive or negative, can spur on a conversation among your loyal following. A good example of this is that some people will screenshot particularly hateful comments (such as those that are racist or sexist) and share them with their following on Twitter in a humorous light. Rather than acting offended, they laugh at how ridiculous the online bullying is that they are receiving. This can evict laughter from the people who have also dealt with similar comments, and sympathy.

Although, this method must be used carefully, be sure that they are truly hateful and bullying comments. Otherwise, you could look bad. A good example of this is people who share comments in this manner, but rather than bullying comments the person was simply letting them know that something they said in the video was racist, sexist, or ableist. Rather than simply accepting or even ignoring the honest criticism the person chooses to mock the commenter publicly.

Along with being sure that it is a truly uncalled for and hateful comment, edit the screenshot and block out the person's name and avatar so that you are not revealing their information. Following this method at all completely depends on your brand. It is more effective when used by individuals targeting a younger audience.

While you can call attention to the negative comments you receive, it is a good idea to almost always keep your interactions with fans positive. You want your audience to know that you appreciate their feedback, and not that you are hostile toward them. While it takes time, try to respond to as many comments as you can. Some comments can be a simple "thank you for watching" or "I appreciate your thoughts," but other times try to go more in-depth and have a full discussion with people in the comments. Be kind, respectful, give what they have considered, and treat them as individuals rather than one whole.

If you have an engaging and relevant conversation with viewers, you can even feature it in your next video. While an audience loves getting comments from you, one thing a loyal audience will most appreciate is if you publicly acknowledge them. It makes them feel special and reaffirms that you care. You can do this by taking a screenshot of their interaction with you, adding it to the video, and addressing them by their username. For instance, you could say "I had a wonderful discussion with CatLover213 last week, and what they said here really got me to thinking..." or "I was asked by DogObsessed500 what my opinion on this subject here, since I am asked this question frequently I decided to take the time to film a video answering your question." You will find that the more you address your audience on a personal level, the more loyal they will feel.

One common misconception is that when you are video marketing that it is only about your content, but this is not true. Instead, you want to head out of your sphere at times to interact with people, whether or not they are a viewer of yours.

On YouTube, you can do this by leaving comments on other people's channel. If you are already a viewer of yours, they will be excited to see that you took the time to watch and comment on their content. If they are not a previous viewer, it will give them the opportunity to discover your channel and possibly become a fan.

When leaving comments on other people's channels, the most important thing to remember is not to spam them. Don't simply say "hi," "good thoughts," or worst yet, "check out my channel!" Nobody wants to interact with someone who is simply out for their own gain and using others as a marketing ploy. Rather, give a comment that is reflective of what was discussed in the video. You want your comment to provide value to the conversation rather than something insincere.

The best way in which you can keep your viewers engaged in the conversation after watching the video is to ask them to participate directly. Don't just rely on them having the idea to comment or "like" your video. People are more likely to feel motivated if you directly ask them at the end of your video, such as "thank you for taking the time to watch. I would appreciate hearing your thoughts. What is your opinion on this matter? Please comment below and let me know!"

You can especially boost the number of comments you receive if you let them know that you will be including your favorite comments in a future video. You could make a video replying to the top five or ten comments. If people know you are planning this, they would want their comment to be included and are likely to come back to your channel to see if their comment was included in your future video.

Lastly, remember to genuinely thank your audience for their likes, subscribes, and comments.

Remember, audience engagement requires a conversation, and a conversation begins by asking your viewers questions.

Chapter 4: Adding Interest and Humor with Music

One of the secrets to successfully utilizing video marketing is to stimulate as many of your viewers' senses as possible. One of the most important senses, in this case, is sound. This doesn't mean you just need to focus on the voice of the person who is doing the talking, but of sound effects and background music, as well. Think about it; this music can play in the person's subconscious for long after they watch your video, bringing your message back to their mind.

Some of the most famous ads throughout history are known for their use of music. Even the Cocoa-Cola commercial from 1971 is still famous for its use of I'd Like to Buy the World a Coke by Hilltop. Some other examples include Amazon Kindle's 2010 commercial including Fly Me Away by Annie Little and Oreo's Wonderfilled commercial from 2013 featuring Owl City.

These commercials are able to live on long after they originally aired because they use music as a tool to draw out emotions from people. The song I'd Like to Buy the World a Coke is not only catchy, but it also offers a feeling of hope and unity. Fly Me Away draws out feelings of sweet happiness, Wonderfilled is full of feelings of nostalgic happiness. Using the right music ingrains your message into people's hearts, which may even last for decades.

Music has many important features in video marketing. Music might add an extra element of entertainment, which will prevent your viewers from becoming bored. It may be used to further your message and the feelings you are trying to convey. Music may also simply be used as quiet background noise, to help the listener to stay focused on what is being said.

If you use music correctly, it can help your audience form an attachment to your videos, making them want to watch further.

First, before we discuss how you can make use of this special tool, it is important to note that you must be careful in the legality of the music you choose. Most music is copyrighted, and if you use one of these songs then YouTube will not only remove your video, but you could potentially face legal action. Thankfully, for those on a tight budget YouTube offers free copyright-free music, which you can use as you like in your videos without worry. You can find this music in your YouTube Dashboard creator's section. There are also other websites on which you can find copyright-free music.

Though, if your brand has some budget to spare, it is well worth hiring a composer to create a song specifically for your use. It may cost a bit, but it is worth it, as you will have music that nobody else has rights to. This means that when someone hears the song or something similar they will immediately remember your brand. Having custom music will also ensure you have the exact sound, tempo, and emotion you are hoping for.

Before you begin to film or edit your video, consider what role you want music to play. You need to decide whether the music will be in the foreground or background, what mood should it evoke, what is the temp, preferably you should know exactly what musical piece or song you are planning on using.

This will ensure that the music fits the video. If you want to discuss technical information with your viewers, then a light underscore is usually better, to help the audience focus on what is being said. But, if you are discussing more broad concepts, then you might choose foreground emotion which draws out more emotion.

When choosing a song or music piece, it is best to pick something where the rhythm flows with the pace of the speech. Sometimes it can be really successful even to allow the music to slowly fade out during an important part of the discussion, before slowly reintroducing it. While effective, it is best not to overuse this technique. Otherwise, it may lose its potency.

You always want to consider who your videos are targeting, and this is the truth when choosing music. For instance, you wouldn't hear a Taylor Swift or One Direction song in commercial targeting seniors. Choose what genre is most likely to appeal to your audience.

A few seconds of music at the beginning and end of videos act as a helpful tool to prepare your viewers to listen, and then to help them feel as if the video is complete when it ends. This music should set the tone of the video and only last for a few seconds.

One of the biggest secrets to using music to add interest for your audience is to make it funny. This can be difficult, and there are many situations it doesn't work. But, if you have the opportunity to use it, then it could pay off.

Example One: Imagine a commercial where you see a couple fighting, and one of them may even threaten divorce. The lighting is dim, and the music sets a slow and ominous tone for what is to come. The camera slowly pans over to the couple, and then you realize they are fighting over who took the last slice of pizza. The lights become brighter, and the music screeches to a halt when the couple realizes that the pizza is their favorite brand of pre-made frozen pizza, that they have more in the freezer, and can make more. It turns out the fight was never actually serious, but a commercial for a common brand of frozen pizza. Using the dark music with the argument catches people's attention, and then the twist at the end makes it funny.

Example Two: In this commercial, various people are being interviewed about their obsession, and how it is getting in the way of their professional and personal lives. The music is somber, and while everyone is talking seriously, what they are saying is a mixture of farce and deadpan. It is overly ridiculous that it is funny. Their "obsession" is actually for a new smartphone game app.

Example Three: The commercial starts with happy and peppy music, which the character is dancing around to. The ad may at first seem as if it is for a new brand of snack, but when the person runs out of their house eating their snack they end up crashing into a car. The sudden accident is such a shock that it suddenly grabs everyone's attention. The next scene is the same character, in the hospital, urging people to buy health insurance. In this commercial, the peppy, happy music contrasts significantly to the somber message, first shocking people and then making them laugh. It is a commercial people are sure to remember.

Lastly, while you can't use copyright music, it is legal to make music parodies. NASA has a wonderful example of this when their interns danced and sang All About that Space in 2014. This was a parody of the popular song, All About that Bass, and it went viral. People love parody music videos, especially when they are done in a fun and unique way.

Whether you choose to use music as background noise, to make a point, to draw out emotion, or to make people laugh, choosing the right music is vital and must be planned before filming.

Chapter 5: Have a Selling Point

One reason in which videos have become so powerful in marketing is that they are much more easily and quickly consumed than written content. Because of this, the use of video marketing has now risen so that eighty percent of companies are using it. Yet, when creating this content, some people may just be waiting for it to go viral.

Yes, going vital is a good perk. In 2017 the company TwirlyGirl experienced going viral due to their funny, unique, and cute YouTube ad. But, they would not have been able to successfully do this if going viral was the only aspect they considered. Instead, they focused on their message, product, and brand. TwirlyGirl was able to create an ad that perfectly matched their brand and utilized their unique strengths; this is why it went viral. Sure, you could go viral for a cute cat video, but if it doesn't further your brand, then there is no point.

Whether or not you have a specific product to sell, every video should have a selling point: your brand. This is more complex than simply showcasing the features of a product, but it is incredibly valuable to include. If your audience understands and knows your brand, then they will feel more comfortable watching your videos, buying products or services, and are more likely to become loyal.

Before you begin to sell your brand, you need to have a full understanding of what your brand and message is. This means that you need to write out a list of what your brand stands for, what its mission is, and what it offers people. If you do not know yourself, then others cannot know you, either. Be specific when writing out your list.

Your message is the way in which you communicate your brand's meaning and persona. Practice elevator pitches, short biographies to include on websites, taglines for business cards. All of these may vary depending on the length, but they all need to have the same core message and be tied together. Most importantly, your message needs to tell people what you offer and how you can help them.

People are hyping up their businesses every day, exaggerating and stretching the truth until nobody knows who to believe. Because of this, you can't simply make claims about your brand that you know to be true; you need to back them up as truth. Share facts about what your brand has been able to accomplish successfully. Your clients will feel confident about choosing your brand if they can trust you.

One of the biggest tools that you will notice large companies successfully utilize is not only having a clear brand but clearly displaying it everywhere. For instance, you usually know an Allstate or State Farm commercial you see it. They have learned what branding works for them, and then they continue to use it on full display. Every time you post a video, no matter what type, you should consider how you can work your brand into it seamlessly. Whether you are looking to sell a product or not, you should constantly be selling your brand.

There are many types of videos in which you can promote yourself. Some people may utilize all of these, or only one. It really depends on your brand and what works. Examine your brand, and then decide which video types you think will most suit it. You should have a good idea since by this point you clearly understand both your brand and your audience, but you can keep track of analytics to be sure which video type is working best.

One of the most powerful options is video testimonials. In fact, WebDam reported that this type of video marketing has an eighty-nine percent success rate. If you have a local business, you can film this yourself, or if you have an online business you can ask people to film them themselves and send the clips in for you to edit and share. People are unlikely to want to do this if they aren't getting anything out of it so you can offer an incentive to the people who send in testimonials. For instance, they could be entered into a giveaway or receive a discount on their next purchase.

Education videos are extremely popular. Whether you are filming a series of videos which showcase your unique industry knowledge or how to use a product, they are likely to be popular. People regularly use YouTube as a free learning tool. The prior example will give people the security of knowing that you truly have the knowledge you claim. People often use the latter example, how to use a product, in deciding whether or not to make a purchase. According to a study, four in five consumers have reported to finding video product demos helpful, which can greatly boost sales.

DIY/Workshop videos are popular, and this can be especially helpful for people who have created businesses which require working with their hands. For instance, a painter could film a workshop series on how to paint with watercolors. At the end of each video, they could either pitch a full painting course which contains additional information or direct their viewers to an online store to buy their paintings.

Vlogs (video blogs) that show a day in people's lives are becoming ever more popular. Some people may find benefit from including occasional vlogs that showcase how they go about their job. Again, this is especially beneficial for those in artistic fields. But, it can be beneficial for other people as well, as it puts a face behind the brand. If they can see the products being produced by real people, just like them, then they can become more loyal.

Videos that showcase who your company is in an overview, backstory, and explain the various aspect of your business are always helpful to add. You don't want these to be your only videos, but if you use them along with other types of videos that can build viewer trust.

Lastly, while fully understanding your brand and being able to communicate it is important when you are trying to sell a product you sell people on supporting your brand, there are other aspects that are important. When you are marketing yourself across multiple websites and social media platforms it is easy for the message to get muddled.

Study your brand's message as a whole, across the entire internet, and on location, if you have one. You want to be sure that your videos contain the same logos, fonts, color scheme, and messages as you convey elsewhere. You want your brand to become recognizable to the point that people can easily recognize your message and brand when they lay eyes upon it.

Chapter 6: Perfect Your Video

Before you film your video, you need to begin by creating a storyboard and either a full script or detailed talking points. If you decide to go the full script route is careful, few people are able to pull this off naturally. It can often come off as fake, which leads to people having a distrust of what you are saying. I prefer to create specific talking points, along with planning out where I want to mention them in the video. This way is often ideal because you don't forget what you want to say, but it still comes off as natural and sincere.

For your storyboard, you should plan out all of the camera angles and footage you will need. This can vary greatly depending on the video type. For instance, if you are filming an interview, you will only need a few camera angles. But, if you are filming a product demo, you will need many different shots to appropriately highly all of the features of the product and the person demonstrating them. Some people will draw these storyboards, others will take photos for reference, or it can even be a simple list that you write out. These stages are important because the more you plan your video beforehand, the less time you will have to spend filming and editing. It will also lend to a more clean and cohesive look.

Some people may choose to use B-roll footage in their videos, which put simply is footage of anything other than your primary subject. This means if you are filming a video explaining your brand, the B-roll footage could be footage of people working around the office, helping customers, and any products being assembled. Then, during editing, you can have the person telling the story of the brand as the main focus, with clips of the company functioning put throughout. When you want to plan the B-roll footage needed during the initial planning phase, you will create your storyboard.

The camera angle is extremely important; there are many angles which are unflattering. You want to put your best image out there, and that includes how you appear on the video. There are three main angles:

Eye Level: Often the most flattering, eye level is frequently used for corporate and professional filming, as it is neutral in how it displays the figure on screens. This angle is clear and straight to the point.

Above Eye Level: Filming with the camera angled from up high down on a person's face is often used to give a person a weak or childlike appearance, which unless you are filming an elaborate commercial, you are unlike to want.

Below Eye Level: Like the previous angle, are unlike to use this one for any professional filming, except commercials. This angle can look intimidating and foreboding, which is not the image you want to project for your brand.

While you will generally stick the eye level for your filming, some people may benefit with the camera raised ever so lightly. You don't want it to be very high, but just slightly higher than eye level may be flattering for some people. For instance, this can prevent people who have thin faces from appearing to have overly prominent bones. Another instance in which this can be helpful is for people who have round faces, as it prevents the look of a double chin.

Along with these three angles, you can also choose a close-up, medium, or wide range. It can often help to get these clips at a variety of ranges. For instance, if you are filming an interview of two people, you can utilize a wide range shot to capture both individuals along with some close-ups to focus on the person who is talking during scenes that are more emotional. You will frequently see this method used in interviews and late night shows.

The way in which you can make use of lighting in filming could fill an entire book. But, there is a specific type of lighting you typically want when creating promotional brand content. You want a light that is bright and shines on your entire face evenly, without shadows or highlights. You can use either natural light or artificial light for this, though unless you have expensive professional photography lights you are likely to get the best look with natural sunlight. For this reason, it is usually best to film when the sun is hitting directly through the windows.

If you decide to go with artificial lighting, be sure that you get lights that emit a cool tone rather than warm. Otherwise, your subject will turn out looking yellow. You will need many lights to hit from various angles. Most often lights are used at all angles for this, to the center, left, and right of the subject, as well as some on ground level, some above head level, and possible some even behind the subject.

Choose either one lighting source or the other, but don't combine them. If you combine both natural and artificial lighting, it usually results in uneven and unflattering lighting. This is true even for advanced videographers.

While nearly every camera has an auto-white balance setting, you might want to customize this. Most cameras will include a manual demonstrating how to reset the white balance, which is the most accurate method. But, if you are unable to do this, many cameras at least offer white balance settings based on the source of lighting. For instance, they can have different ones for sun, overcast, fluorescent, et cetera.

Additional Tips:

- Always use a tripod when possible. You may think someone can hold the camera steady for you, but the slightest movement or tremor will be extremely visible on many cameras. Setting the camera on a hard surface, such as a table, is also not ideal as you cannot adjust the angle very well.

Although, if you are promoting some sort of sporting and outdoors brand, you may have to film without a tripod. For instance, if you sell mountain bikes, you may need to go outdoors and film on the move. In this case, GoPro cameras are widely regarded as the absolute best sporting and outdoor cameras. While they don't have the best audio capabilities, they are amazing for getting action shots.

- When deciding on a location to film, look at the background. If you are standing in front of a plain wall, it will most likely be boring. Look for a visually stimulating but laid-back atmosphere. For instance, if you see someone sitting at a desk, is unlikely to distract you from the person speaking, but it is more interesting to look at than a blank wall. Similarly, try to avoid filming in locations where there is action going on behind you, such as people walking by. Seeing the constant change in atmosphere is likely to distract the viewer. You want a clean and pleasant background that is static but visually pleasing.

- Don't zoom in for close-ups. This leads to poorer quality video and can create a shaky look to the video. When at all possible, if you need a close-up angle physically move closer to the subject.

- There are many cameras that are enabled with decent microphones, though GoPro isn't one of them. But, if you are using a microphone built into a camera, you will need to ensure that you are close enough to the camera to be well-heard. Otherwise, you will need to invest in a microphone. Thankfully, you can get pretty decent microphones between twenty and seventy dollars.

When editing your footage, you can use a wide range of programs. Most computers come with built-in video editing software, but this is highly limited, and you are unable to customize it nearly as much. If you decide to buy video editing software, you can find many YouTube tutorials of learning to use it simply. Some common choices include Premiere Pro, After Effects, Final Cut Pro, Avid Media Composer, DaVinci Resolve, Lightworks, Autodesk Smoke, and Sony Vegas.

If after you film your video you find the white balance isn't as balanced as you thought, and the video has a blue or yellow tint, then you should be able to color correct the footage until it looks even.

You can play around with including text, graphics, and effects, but keep these limited. When used in excess these have an unprofessional air. But, a graphic or two, a logo, and some text here or there in moderation can add a wonderful element. Explore successful video marketing of other businesses to get an idea of what works and what doesn't.

Lastly, the important editing secret is to film and repeatedly edit, if needed. The longer you practice filming end editing, the less frequently you will have to redo your work. But, in the beginning, especially you may simply have to film your footage multiple times and try editing it a few times. You want the video you share to be the best it can be to represent your brand properly.

You want to give your video every possible chance for success, and to do this, you may need to film and edit it multiple times.

Chapter 7: Gain Video Shares

Some people may think it is simple vanity when you want to get more shares, comments, and likes on social media. But, for your business to excel you need your video marketing to be successful, and this means you need people to share your work. After all, the way videos go viral is by word of mouth.

Even if your video content doesn't go viral, the more social media attention, and therefore views, it receives the more profit you can gain from it.

Sure, everyone says strong content will do the work for you, and this is true to an extent, but that is not all that is required for success. Having a good understanding of social media and how to utilize it to grab people's attention in the sea of posts from friends and celebrities is also needed.

One way in which you can greatly boost its effectiveness on social media is with the headline. A strong headline can be the difference between dozens of views and thousands. Try to choose a catchy title; one that is between six and eight words is often effective. Using numbers, such as in the very title of this book 7 Video Marketing Secrets can help, as can use words that are tied to strong emotions or actions.

But, it is imperative that you are completely honest with the title of the video and deliver what you promise. If you don't, this is known as click bait and is highly looked down upon. People who produce clickbait are eventually looked down upon as dishonest, and people no longer trust their content.

While you should do everything, you can to market your video correctly, there is little you can do on your own unless you already have thousands of followers. Sure, you could get lucky and become one of those thirty-day success stories. But, even if that is possible, we need to create solid plans for growth in case our company doesn't become famous overnight.

This is where social media influencers come in. These are people who have a high social media following and know how to use it. Marketing your business with an influencer not only improves awareness of your business, but it also increases audience engagement, traffic, and can boost your brand's trustworthiness. You may like the idea of naturally growing your social media influence yourself, but if you are trying to become a success anytime in the near future, it can greatly help to hire a social media influencer.

In fact, social influencers are only becoming more powerful in business. You can now regularly see celebrities, such as Beyoncé, hired by companies to promote them on social media. While it is unlikely you will be able to afford a celebrity, someone who has high influence in your target audience can greatly increase your business. The statistics on this are actually really exciting:

- During 2017 searches including the term 'influencer marketing' increased by three-hundred and twenty-five percent.

- This is continuing to grow as people become more distrustful of traditional advertisements. Approximately sixty-six percent of marketing departments hope to increase their influence on marketing budget over the following year.

- Marketing departments are expected to invest an average of twenty-five thousand to fifty thousand dollars into social media influencer marketing this year.

- This has been incredibly successful, and in general marketers can seven dollars and sixty-five cents in revenue for each dollar they spend on influencer marketing.

- The most popular platform for influencer marketing is Instagram, which facilitated in over twelve million brand sponsored posts by influencers during 2017. This figure is expected to double in 2018.

- Another study revealed that forty percent of Twitter users had made purchases as a direct result of a post from an influencer on Twitter.

You should know who exactly your audience is. For instance, if yours is working mothers in their 30's and 40's with a focus on healthy living, then you will need an influencer who can reach that audience. Obviously, a teen lifestyle influencer would not benefit your brand.

In order to find an influencer in your target market, you will need to search common terms used by your audience on Facebook, Twitter, Instagram, and YouTube. If you have two or three audiences who your product applies to, then you should look for influencers in those areas, as well. Prioritize your top selling audience, and then look more from there.

There are several ways in which you can ask an influencer to help you. The most common ones include sponsored posts, guest blogging, becoming an affiliate, reviews, collaborations on events, and giving the product to influencers to discuss.

Remember, never message an influencer ask them to do you a favor by discussing your brand. They worked hard to build an audience, and it is insulting to ask them to do it for free. Instead, pay them for their services just as you expect to be paid.

There are multiple options to hire a social media influencer, some of these are:

- Hootsuite
  specifically made for managing a variety of social media platforms, Hootsuite makes it simple to both manage your

own social media pages and find an influencer. You can get a thirty-day free trial first to test out the program, so if it doesn't work, you won't lose a thing. With Hootsuite, you can easily view relevant conversations to your field and find social media influencers.

- FollowerWonk
  Free when used with your Twitter account, FollowerWonk will help you find influencers by searching for specific keywords on their profiles and bio. You can even customize this further if you want to specify their location.

- This will let you find the influencers and see their number of followers, social authority, account age, and a number of tweets.

- BuzzSumo
  This website is made specifically for promoting yourself on social media, finding, and hiring social media influencers. They make it simple to find influencers around any topic or location, analyze how influential they are, and reach out to hire them. They have a seven-day free trial, which may not be as long as some of the earlier mentioned websites, but BuzzSumo is a seriously powerful option if you want to hire the right social influencers.

- TrendSpottr
  Created by the same people from Hootsuite, TrendSpottr is perfect if Instagram is your target audience's social network for choice. With this website, you can easily track and analyze influencers, videos, photos, and tags.

- Google
  if all else fails; you can always try a Google search. It might take longer and be more difficult to analyze, but you might

come across some LinkedIn pages or websites to relevant social media influencers.

While you may be able to grow your business and YouTube channel on your own, eventually, if you hire a social media influencer you will find that your brand's presence will grow much more quickly. The studies are clear, on average you can make eight times of what you spend with a social media influencer. So, why not try it out?

Conclusion

While it may take dedication and hard work to utilize video marketing and grow a YouTube channel, it is well worth it. Not only can YouTube, and video marketing in general, help you to increase your income, boost brand awareness, and help you communicate directly with your target audience, but it can also be a business in and of itself. More and more people are becoming YouTubers, where their job is literally to make content for their viewers.

Whichever of these goals you hope to attain, the seven secrets to knowing your audience, keeping your message simplified, adding humor, keeping your viewers engaged, detailing your selling point, perfecting your video, and hiring a social media influencer can help you grow your business and channel.

Thank you for reading *7 Video Marketing Secrets*. Now that you have all of the tools needed for success, please go forward with confidence.

Erich M. Tolman

www.ingramcontent.com/pod-product-compliance
Lightning Source LLC
Chambersburg PA
CBHW030545220526
45463CB00007B/2980